BETWEEN RIVERS AND SEA

THE RIBBLE ESTUARY

OVER

TWO CENTURIES

BY

FRANK BAMFORD

Publishing and Photography
by
Colin Bamford

First published in 2009 by
Colin Bamford, 11 Ridge Avenue, Hale Barns, Altrincham, WA15 0AY

Copyright Frank Bamford 2009
ISBN 978 -0-9562143-0-0
Ordnance Survey Licence number 100048970

Typeset by Colin Bamford

Printed by Silprint Units 4-5, Pitt Street Business Centre, Pitt Street,
Keighley, West Yorkshire, BD21 4PF

BETWEEN RIVERS AND SEA
THE RIBBLE ESTUARY OVER TWO CENTURIES

1.   INTRODUCTION

Across the wide spread of the bay formed by the Ribble Estuary, Southport and Lytham gaze at each other across a five miles stretch of sea which seems deceivingly less. In reality, of course, to travel by land from one end of the bay to the other involves a journey of nearly 30 miles taking well over an hour, yet no bridge has ever been built across the river seaward of Penwortham in spite of a number of tentative plans. In the 19th century the two small towns on the tips of the estuary, separately exploiting their situations facing the open sea, became the notable seaside resorts of Southport and Lytham St Annes.

The people who have lived along the coasts of this estuary have always of course been somewhat remote from the rest of England, with no close centre of population or industry apart from the developing resorts at its tips. In the 18th century even Preston, an important gateway between the North of England and the Midlands, was a quite modest town until steam power brought the cotton industry most substantially to it well into the 19th century. So inevitably agriculture was by far the dominant way of life with fishing in support.

Inevitably, too, the folk who lived by the river sought to make the most of their modest neighbouring contacts, even when these lived across the water, both for trade and for social purposes. We shall learn something of how these cross-Ribble contacts were made before human invention made them easier and very different.

In the two centuries since life was so simple, the major inventions and developments in the wider realm of England effectively brought about such huge changes that we can distinguish major AGES, often overlapping. So before we examine the consequences of these national changes for the people who have lived by the Ribble Estuary we need to consider locally the various AGES involved.

AGE OF THE EARLY ROADS

Until the 18th century, connections between villages and towns were little more than mud tracks along which people walked or rode on horses or a few stage coaches. Goods were carried mainly on horses, often piled high. The use of horse-drawn carts required better roads.

In the 18th century men like MacAdam improved road surfaces with finance provided by private businessmen or local councils who developed the turnpike roads, so named because of the 'pike' devices used to control traffic. These roads were essentially the means of travel from one village to another. Tarleton was close to the turnpike road, which is now the A59, going from Preston through Longton towards Ormskirk. (At this point Southport did not exist.)

AGE OF THE RIVERS

England has always possessed a huge advantage over the princip
countries of Northern Europe in the shape of its heavily indented coastlir
and its many long rivers. All parts of the country have therefore enjoye
not only remarkable access to each other but also to neighbouring cour
tries and indeed the rest of the world. With the use of simple boats, drive
by wind power and horse power, trade was developed, moving good
faster than could be achieved by horse power on land.

There was, however, a downside to the existence of the rivers ir
that they constituted barriers between local communities, which ofte
could only be bridged by expensive constructions or hazardous crossing
on foot or in small boats.

In the Ribble estuary the situation was somewhat complicated by th
existence of the River Douglas (or Asland) which still joins the south ban
of the Ribble between Hesketh Bank and Longton. By the early 18th Cer
tury the development of industry in the north of England and elsewher
had encouraged the development of coal mining for the heating of homes
workshops and indeed factories in the expanding industrial areas and th
transport of coal from Lancashire became of huge importance. In 1720 a
Act of Parliament authorised a group of businessmen to make the Rive
Douglas navigable to the estuary of the Ribble and so to the sea. This
task was completed by 1740.

AGE OF THE CANALS

From around the middle of the 18th century, as the growth of industry
accelerated, the advantage of water transport became so substantial anc
so vital to trade and industry that it became profitable for some business
enterprises to construct artificial rivers in the form of canals, beginning
with the Duke of Bridgewater's canal constructed to take coal from his
mine at Worsley to heat the houses in the great cotton industry area
around Manchester by 1760. Later this pioneering waterway was ex
tended south of Manchester to proceed, by a winding route along the con-
tour lines to avoid building locks, to the Mersey estuary near Birkenhead
and Liverpool.

By 1780 an even more tremendous enterprise had begun, to construct the greatest canal of all, the Leeds and Liverpool, to connect the
industrial areas of West Yorkshire and Lancashire by the quickest route to
the port of Liverpool and so to the oceans and continents of the world. By
the end of the century the Leeds and Liverpool Company had taken over
the River Douglas Navigation to provide an outlet to the Ribble estuary at
Hesketh Bank.

By 1820 the Leeds and Liverpool came within 5 miles of the resort of Southport at the southern tip of the Ribble estuary basin and strongly stimulated the town's early development. A canal link to Manchester via the Bridgewater Canal was also established around this time.

Thus by the early 19th century the coasts and great rivers of the country had been quite systematically linked to each other by the new canals so that Britain had become indeed a lively patchwork of waterways. The Ribble Estuary was directly linked to this canal system via the River Douglas. Most importantly it was linked to Lancashire coal which was vital for heating homes and businesses.

THE AGE OF THE TRAIN

Such, however, was the break-neck speed of the application of technology to transport, as well as to industry, that in 1830 the Age of the Train was begun by the opening of the passenger line from Liverpool to Manchester. Within 20 or 30 years the industrial areas of the north were crisscrossed with railways as well as canals and rivers. Preston became an important railway junction. When the Great Exhibition of 1851 was opened in Hyde Park in London, the organisers were astonished at the multitude of working people who came down from the industrial north by train to visit it. Some well-to-do people even feared a bloody revolution but the visitors were all well behaved and respectful. Certainly the railway train was hugely revolutionary in the social life of England.

As we shall see, a few decades more would see the train reaching even the quiet areas of England by the Ribble in the south-west of Lancashire.

THE AGE OF STEAM AND INDUSTRY

Overlapping the Ages of the Canal and the Train and closely involved in their development, was the all-important Age of Steam and indeed of Industry. For centuries the textile industries of Lancashire and Yorkshire had been based on the use of the power of water which came down from the Pennines to form the very rivers which further down were so useful for transportation. The application of this power to improving machinery was the first major step in modernisation. Late in the 18th century the application of steam power first to spinning and some decades later to weaving, enabled much larger machines to be located away from the running water of the hillsides so that Manchester developed from being a city only of commerce to be the site of huge cotton spinning mills.

A little later Preston, too, became a great manufacturing town, so that its population doubled by 1870, leaping ahead fastest in the mid-century decades, a development of huge significance for the Ribble estuary where changes were being made to improve access by boats to Preston.

Cotton weaving, a more complex operation, with more scope for individual attention, would take much longer to mechanise, so much weaving would continue in people's homes or workshops and small factories well into the second half of the 19th century. We shall hear of a sizeable factory on each side of the Ribble in the latter period.

THE AGE OF THE CAR

The Age of the Car began early in the 20th century and was becoming quite dominant by the Second World War to the extent that the railways became partly redundant while roads needed revolutionary improvement. The Beeching Report of 1964 killed many local lines including the direct line from Preston to Southport, although the Southport to Liverpool line mercifully survived.

The arrival of motor cars revolutionised personal and freight transport after two world wars, making it possible for both to move much further and faster.

THE AGE OF FLIGHT

From the Second World War onwards, air travel became increasingly available to many people making overseas holidays to the sun extremely popular by 1960 to 1970 with a consequential huge reduction in business for the seaside resorts around the Ribble estuary.

2.   THE WAYWARD RIBBLE AND ITS MANAGEMENT

From the Age of the Rivers the Ribble estuary was central to the lives of the few thousands of people who lived along its banks, from Lytham to Freckleton in the North and from Southport to Hutton to the South, all too far from the historical town of Preston to be closely influenced by it, indeed too far from anywhere with many inhabitants to be substantial communities and for there to be almost any kind of life other than agricultural until the Ages of Canals, the Train and Steam brought greater contacts of people, transport and industry.

The great river was of course also a substantial barrier between the neighbours who lived on its opposite banks, but other neighbours were so far away that there was always a considerable incentive to cross the water to make and maintain friendly contacts and to carry out a certain amount of trade mainly of agricultural products. Such crossings were not perhaps as difficult as one might suppose since the volume of water coming down the Ribble was never very large across the wide mouth of its estuary and seems to have been reduced by the growth of contaminating and water consuming industry on its path through industrial Lancashire.

Thus, both on foot and little boat, crossings of the shallow river were quite common, depending on the tide. They were not without hazard particularly because of the changing pattern of sand on the river bed, which caused the several channels to move from time to time and made the employment of guides most advisable. Indeed, over long periods of the 18th and 19th centuries, ships going in and out of Preston harbour were well advised to employ them.

There were certain recommended customary routes across the estuary, from Freckleton or Warton to Hesketh Bank or Longton, for instance. For a long time Warton to Longton was a favoured route; also for long periods were other journeys from Lytham to Hesketh Bank and Longton. The use of guides was advisable for all but the most experienced travellers.

The whole physical pattern was greatly complicated by the existence of the other important river which flowed into the Ribble between Hesketh Bank and Longton i.e. the Douglas (or Asland). The mid 19th century map shows that at that time the main Douglas current flowed straight out just past Hall Green and the end of Marsh Lane near Longton, crossing over, with some deviation, to near to the Naze near Freckleton so that crossings of the Ribble from these points would have been fairly straightforward, with journeys between Longton and Hesketh Bank quite simple although, of course, involving crossing the Douglas at one of several points.

Downstream of the Ribble from this area there were three principal streams which were not reliably stable, since, as we have noted, the mov-

ing water tended to alter the underlying sand pattern quite substantiall
Two of the streams passed near Lytham, which was for many years
smallish port of some importance.

Well before the Age of the Canals, the Douglas was developed
carry coal and other products from around Wigan via Hesketh Bank to th
Fylde and elsewhere across the Ribble. A special Act of Parliament wa
passed as early as 1720 to enable the necessary clearance work to b
carried out to make the river navigable, an operation which was complete
by 1740.

A substantial business of exporting coal and later a variety of indu
trial products was developed coupled with the importation from Ireland of
number of farm products. Boats from Wigan crossed from Hesketh Bar
to Lytham and Freckleton and ferried passengers as well as goods. Th
was undoubtedly of major importance for forging and maintaining contac
between the banks of the Ribble. It continued as a thriving connection fc
100 years or more.

The idea of dredging and 'training' the river by constructing guid
walls so as to create a deeper and narrower single channel had been dis
cussed as a business proposition since early in the 19th century, but th
chief financial incentive seemed to have been in respect of reclaiming lan
which could be sold for agriculture. Yet as the early decades passed, the
manufacturing industry of West Lancashire was developing fast, particu
larly in the form of great cotton spinning mills in the Preston area. So th
prospect soon emerged of improving the transit of the Ribble to such a
major extent that many more and larger ships should reach Preston fror
the sea, importing coal, cotton and agricultural products and exporting
manufactured products. Local businessmen subscribed heavily to this
project in three phases organised by the First, Second and Third Ribble
Navigation Companies in the periods 1806-1838, 1838-1853 and 1853
1883. Significantly, the first company was originally owned and finance
mainly by the Ribble landowners.

By mid-century considerable progress had been made in dredging
the main channel of the river downstream to the area of the Naze nea
Freckleton and also in building guiding walls in the same length of water
Two separate streams persisted down to Lytham, both of them going
close to the town and its dock.

By 1850 over 900 acres of land had been reclaimed, worth in tota
some £13,000, of which nearly two thirds were sold for £8,000. The most
important areas were around Hesketh Bank (436 acres) with the local
landowner, Sir Fermor Hesketh, as the principal purchaser, and Clifton
(146 acres).

As further improvements were made to the Ribble in subsequent
decades, the area of reclaimed land continued to grow, so that by 1880
over a further mile of new land off Hesketh Bank had been reclaimed in

Note the major streams going close to Lytham

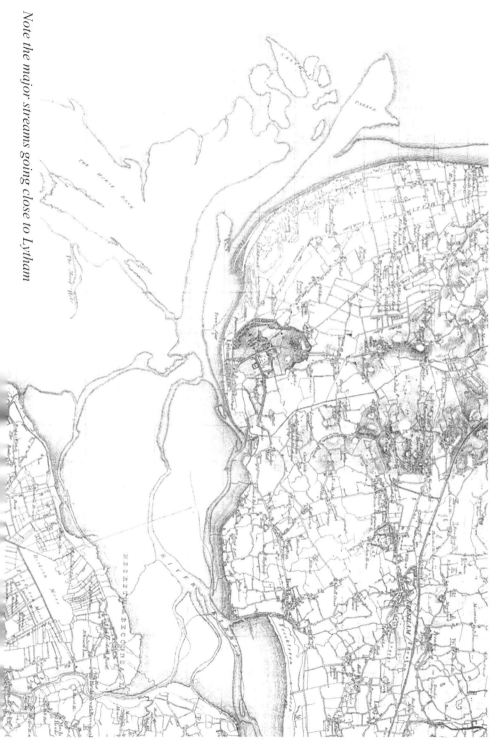

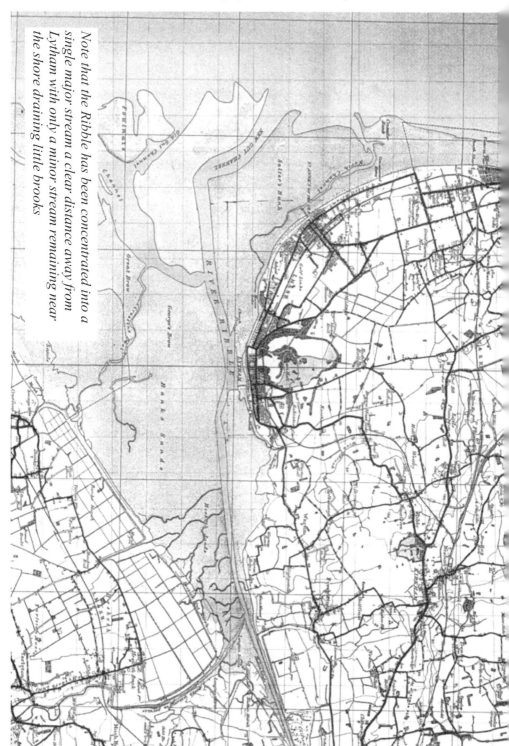

Note that the Ribble has been concentrated into a single major stream a clear distance away from Lytham with only a minor stream remaining near the shore draining little brooks

less than half a century. Typically, the new land, with its black soil, was very fertile and productive of basic agricultural products such as potatoes. By the end of the century new embankments had been constructed near Marshside and Crossens, which were 1¼ miles west of the coastline of the early part of the century. The impact of this extension of dry or marshy land extended as far as Southport where in the 1870's the sea effectively began to desert its close sandy beach right down to Ainsdale.

The following pages from the 2001 book 'Back to the Sea' conveniently summarise the story of Southport in the first half of the 19th century.

The ancient parish of North Meols was centred in what is now the village of Churchtown with its church, hall and two coaching inns, just a few miles from today's Southport centre. As the attractions of sea-bathing became more evident and accessible to a small but growing fraction of the Lancashire population it became apparent that the beach at Southport was more attractive if only because it was less exposed to Ribble mud, and the first little hotel was built in 1798 near what is now the south end of Lord Street.

By 1800 the population of the whole North Meols area was no more then 2,500 with only a few hundreds in what is now the town of Southport in a few score houses built along the sand hills in the area which became Lord Street. For the next twenty years growth was quite slow so that in 1821 North Meols included only just over 3,000 inhabitants of which Southport probably accounted for about 500.

It was in the following twenty years that a great spurt developed with North Meols rising to over 8,000 and Southport accounting for 2161 residents and 1185 visitors, according to a contemporary report. By 1851 the numbers had grown steadily to 9,300 for all North Meols including a grand total of 4,200 for Southport.

How then do we account for this accelerated growth from 1820 to 1850? Well, it is of course partly a reflection of the growth of the industrial population of Lancashire with the associated rise in wealth of the owning and managerial classes. But, above all, it was a question of access. In this period the only semblance of the commercial provision of passenger transport was the skeletonic stage coach system. There was still no decent road even into Southport, although a few stage coaches made their way there. However, the industry — driven creation of the canal network for moving materials and goods created a spin-off benefit for those quite few individuals who could afford the time and money to travel to the coast.

Even so, the benefit was quite limited during the decades from the 1770's during which the Leeds-Liverpool Canal was progressively opened reaching Blackburn, for instance, in 1810. It was only when the link to Manchester was completed in 1820 by the opening of the branch from Wigan to Leigh that the passenger traffic to Southport really began to take off.

From inland Lancashire towns like Wigan, Blackburn, Burnley and Manchester itself, people were able to disembark at Scarisbrick and transfer to horse-drawn carriages and carts for the five-mile trip to the seaside. Visitors also came from the Liverpool area which had its own seaside attractions. It was a very slow means of transport but it did widen the range of possibilities.

Thus Southport itself had changed but little by the 1820's with buildings confined to what is now the southern half of Lord Street with substantial houses along the eastern side and a row behind it. By 1850, however when the railway age (of which much more in the next chapter) had barely begun, both sides of Lord Street had been quite fully developed. A private promenade had been built for a quarter of a mile from the south to reach the Victoria Baths with new links to Lord Street, i.e. Neville Street and Sea Bank Road. East Bank Street, Chapel Street and Hoghton Street were developing, as well as the area south of East Bank Street.

It is important to stress at this point that the only people who could visit Southport before the railway age, let alone build houses and settle there, were those who were relatively affluent enough to be able to spare the significant amount of time and money to overcome the problem of the distance from the large industrial areas and towns. This distance was too great for the mill owners to commute on a regular basis, yet not too far for a small number of them to establish holiday and retirement homes. Already, however, the tone was set for the characteristically large scale of the impressive dwellings, which have dominated the heart of the town until today.

An astonishing token of the wealth of the local inhabitants is that in the early 1850's when the population of Southport, including visitors, was barely 5000 and that of the whole North Meols parish some 10,000, they were planning to build an elegant classical town hall which was in fact opened in 1854. Such civic pride was typical of the Lancashire cotton towns in the Victorian period but rarely at such an early stage in local development.

Of course the new town hall presided in the middle of Lord Street which, following the lines of the sand hills on which it was originally built along the sides of the marshy trough between had already attained something of its spacious elegant appearance, consistent with the wealth of the town's early inhabitants, for which it has become famous.

By this time Southport, which had been reached by the railway in 1846, had become an extremely popular seaside resort, where large numbers of people who had benefited from the prosperity of the Lancashire cotton industry had built large houses, mansions even. Later, working operatives from the cotton factories also enjoyed the new resort in their newly granted "wakes weeks" for which the railway companies provided many excursion trains.

The loss of its close beach reduced Southport's attractions from the 1870's and 1880's and so encouraged holiday makers to travel to Blackpool, which was much less easy of access. Although favoured with a branch off the Fleetwood railway line from Preston in 1846, Blackpool did not benefit from a direct line along the coast via Lytham until 1876 – a sign of its fresh advantage over Southport which soon encouraged the creation of St Annes so Blackpool itself did not overtake Southport in numbers of holiday visitors until the First World War.

Southport Town Hall built 1854

The project of sufficiently improving the Ribble channel was becoming more difficult as the 19th century proceeded, essentially because of increasing competition from other ports. Notably even Fleetwood had been considered important enough to attract a direct railway line from Preston in 1840. Liverpool was always a huge competitor to Preston in the Railway Age. With much more shipping on the seas and oceans in the Industrial Age, with steam becoming swiftly of major importance, ships were continually getting bigger and the Ribble was always needing greater depth. The port of Preston also suffered from its tidal character which limited the hours it could operate, especially with larger ships. In any event, the port required major wet dock facilities.

By 1880 it became clear that the local businessmen who had funded and managed the river and its improvement work in recent decades could no longer afford the substantial funds which the ongoing project required. So the Preston Council took it over from 1883, built a huge wet dock – the biggest in the world – and kept it going, with many ups and *downs, for almost a century until the economics of the modern world proved too much for it. Even the vital coal trade was falling as coal fired power stations became fewer and the Irish trade also decreased.*

Aerial view of the new dock looking east. The Ribble coming from the south had been diverted to make way for the dock. The entry lock can be plainly seen towards the bottom of the picture.

So Preston dock finally closed in 1982 when the Council decided it could no longer fund the £200,000 annual loss which was the cost of the ongoing dredging work in the Ribble.

Busy traffic on the new dock c1920

The towns and villages on the banks of the Ribble estuary were all significantly affected by the long 19th century battle to modify and control its eccentricities within the varying socio-economic conditions of the developing ages.

We will consider in turn the story of each of the more significant places, starting with Longton on the south bank, which stands opposite Freckleton on the north.

3.   TOWNS AND VILLAGES BY THE RIBBLE – SOUTH BANK
LONGTON

Longton is an ancient village four miles south of Preston on the A59. It is truly a peculiarly "long town" stretching originally in a long strip for almost two miles from New Longton in the east almost to the Ribble in the west. This strange configuration appears to have been largely caused by the existence of a ridge of land in the central village area, which made building difficult elsewhere. However, it seems likely that there was some ancient attraction to the east which caused an early road to be established from there westward to the river with its potential for travel elsewhere along its banks on either side. On the other hand, a study of early maps of Lancashire and neighbouring areas suggests that the need for contact with the west coast, the river and the sea caused a number of somewhat parallel east/west roads to be created on one of which stood Longton at

View across the Ribble to Freckleton and Warton. Two centuries ago the whole area was covered by the river at high tide. This is the beginning of the Ribble Way Path to the right.

the junction on the road going south from Preston.

The narrow strip of the village has always been composed of three parts. To the east the houses are all strung along Chapel Lane. To the west a similar strip lines Marsh Lane ending in an old inn called the Dolphin, which has taken over the title of the Ferry House, although in the 19th century there was a simple ferry house a little nearer the river which then ran just a few yards away. Between these two flanking strips is the central village area, also clustered around a street which is now naturally part of the A59 towards Southport and Liverpool, but by-passed by the great volume of traffic. This was also quite a narrow shape until expanded substantially sidewards by middle class suburban housing in recent decades.

Along this 'Long Town' strip some 1,000 people lived by 1891, roughly equally divided among its three parts, with Marsh Lane slightly the largest, a total which resulted from a considerable and surprising increase between 1801 and 1821. The actual census figure for Longton in 1841 showed a total population of 1,700 but this included the inhabitants of tiny

The Dolphin Inn which claims to have been 'The Ferry House',
which was originally a few hundred yards from this picture above.

villages or hamlets around such as Walmer Bridge, Hall Green and Hall Carr Lane, all quite close to the River Douglas.

According to the 1891 census the people of Longton were unsurprisingly still engaged mainly in farming, with the land close to Marsh Lane still divided into narrow strips of land dating from the Middle Ages. Indeed the strip pattern north of Marsh Lane extended eastwards along the main village street, although the strips became wider as the houses became grander. The local people lived almost entirely on the produce of these strips, no doubt with certain grazing rights on nearby land, subject of course to trading with neighbours close and far. Longton people were fortunate to have avoided the Enclosure movement which had prepared land in much of England for large scale farming.

There were, however, still a surprisingly large number of weavers. The mechanisation of cotton spinning by steam power from the end of the 18th century had clearly made ample supplies of yarn available for weaving, which was only more slowly converted to factory operation. Many hand-loom weavers still worked at home until the middle of the 19th century but there were increasing numbers of workshops and small factories as the size of machines grew steadily. In fact Longton itself had a substantial weaving mill at one of its close satellite villages, Walmer Bridge, a mile or so along the Liverpool Road. A small mill there seems to have been driven in the 18th century by water power from Walmer Brook running into the River Douglas nearby, but certainly by around mid 19th century a large factory was driven by steam, as our 1860's picture with its striking chimney shows. At this time some 300 people were employed there, some of them walking from Marsh Lane no doubt. There is a remnant of the stream in the middle of Walmer Bridge –

The Mill at Walmer Bridge

the name of the village would seem to show that long ago the brook was a more obvious local feature.

Although quite poor working people lived in all three main parts of Longton, their principal community was centred in Marsh Lane where a Methodist Chapel was built in 1720 with a school following soon afterwards. In 1841 the census showed some 40 people in Marsh Lane classified as weavers. It is possible that a few were able to work in new workshops and factories not only in Walmer Bridge but as far away as Preston, but transport problems would have been severe until later in the century. In 1876 a local reminiscence records that a Wesleyan school banquet attracted some 300 people to tea, and it appears that people were permitted to gather on the lawn at Grove House at the Marsh Lane end of the village where the Wilkins, owners of the principal local brewery, lived. Not far from there a Co-operative store was built early in the 20th century.

There were in fact two breweries quite close together in Marsh Lane. In addition to the Wilkins' factory, there was the so-called Longton Brewery. Both of these were quite close to the Methodist Chapel, some of whose members were seriously embarrassed by the closeness and made life somewhat difficult for the Wilkins who helped to support the Chapel, despite their close connection to the Anglican church in Longton where the family tomb rests. These breweries were the only local industrial establishments apart from the brickworks mentioned below and the mill at Walmer Bridge.

CHAPEL AND BREWERIES TOWARDS THE EASTERN END OF MARH LANE

Early Methodist Chapel built 1807

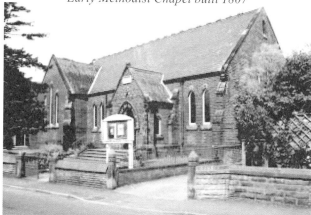

Today's Victorian Methodist Chapel

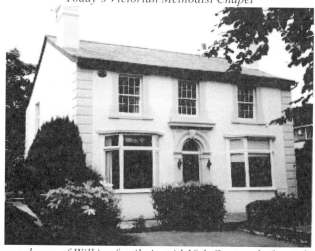

Plumpton House, home of Wilkins family in mid 19th Century before taking over Grove House—see plan on page 24 showing the Grove

Modern nursing home on site of Wilkins Brewery

The site of the other 'Longton Brewery' a hundred yards west of the Wilkins Brewery

The inn just round the end of Marsh Lane on the Liverpool Road

The local Church of England was, and remains, situated at the other end of the village where a strikingly large mid-Victorian church, with school nearby, replaced an 18th century one. In the 20th century, as the population of the village grew and Victorian wealth influenced local trade, the shopping centre of gravity moved to the nearby area. The Co-operative organisation built a substantial shop there, moving from the other end of the village in 1945. Local individual food shops were established near the crossroads between the main street and Chapel Lane. In 1927 Booths, the grocers opened its tenth shop in one of the houses at the beginning of Chapel Lane, expanding into the neighbouring houses later, taking over the Co-op store in 1982 and finally in 2001 building its own moderate sized supermarket on the site of the old Mansion House a short distance down the main village street. In the 21st century this store dominates local food shopping and with some 150 staff is the largest employer in the area. This store has a well patronised café and serves as something of a local community centre.

In the late Victorian period, this main street had in fact increasingly changed into an upper middle class area, particularly on the northern side with a series of major houses, including the Mansion House, the Manor House and the residences of the chief local doctor and the Church of England parson. The latter stood in wide grounds where today two other large houses with substantial gardens are accommodated as well as the original residence. Close by, Shirley Lane leads to a huge area of middle class houses developed in post-war decades, the Age of the Car, which caused the village population to be more than doubled since 1950. This area is now a typical modern dormitory suburb with only a handful of shops and no school. The principal school is now in a modern building on School Lane, beyond the other side of the main Liverpool Road, which replaced an earlier one in the same area, which was itself replaced by an upper middle class housing area at the end of the 20th century.

A Roman Catholic Church and school were established several hundred yards up Chapel Lane. The old Methodist school on Marsh Lane no longer operates. The result of all this development is that many of the children of Longton have quite long journeys to school, causing significant traffic jams twice a day around the village.

A particularly remarkable and endearing feature of Longton is its endowment of no less than four old pubs along the 200 yards stretch of its main street. Two of them at least, one at each end, the Golden Ball and The Ram's Head, were no doubt originally coaching inns, clear evidence of the village's position on the road from Preston to Liverpool (and Southport in the last two centuries). Even more striking, perhaps, is that yet another old coaching inn, The Anchor, remains at Hutton, only two miles along the road to Preston.

The somewhat late arrival of the railway in Longton in 1882, th
story of which is told in a following chapter, made it possible for the vi
lage's principal industry to develop, i.e. bricks and tile making with cla
extracted from two great quarries close to the Liverpool Road. The work
had its own siding from the railway station area which facilitated the des
patch of its products. The closure of the railway in 1964 seemed to coir
cide with the exhaustion of good quality clay so the factory closed an
eventually the whole area was converted into a much valued nature re

Ordinance Survey Map showing Longton Bridge Station and the
Brickworks

*Site of the
Brick and
Tile Works
next to
Longton
Bridge
Station*

serve, after proposals for housing in the area had been much reduced b
public opinion.
 In the modern age of the car, traffic in Longton would have become hor-
rific if the A59 by-pass had not been constructed, running from the Ancho
at Hutton to Much Hoole. As it is, the A59 provides good communicatior
north towards Preston and beyond and south towards Southport and indeed towards central Lancashire. It is a valuable asset for an essentially
residential village with no industry whose people enjoy good housing and
need to travel to work.
 The next chapter on Hesketh Bank (no more than two miles away
as the crow flies), will cover the detailed story of the 18th and 19th water
connections between that village and Longton, but it has to be noted here

that there were ferries and fords in those years between the Marsh Lane tip of Longton across to the Naze near Freckleton, as well as to Hesketh Bank and also from the Hoole and Hall Carr Lane areas to the same places. There may well also have been boats going to and from Lytham.

A century ago, anyone leaving the Golden Ball, for long owned by the Wilkins family, could turn left and pass a bank in the front room of a house close to the mouth of Marsh Lane where four tiny cottages are enclosed by a low wall bearing the identification "Malt Kiln Cottages 1839" which no doubt used to house workers at the Wilkins Brewery. The large impressive house nearby, with the Methodist chapel towering over its attractive garden, bears the much earlier date of 1750 and the title "Park Farm".

If a visitor to the inn turned right on leaving, he might have found work at the local windmill 100 yards along, or possibly the railway station a little further along or the brick and tile works adjacent to it. Within a mile was the weaving factory at Walmer Bridge. Across the road from the Golden Ball stood the village's first Cooperative store, now a major hardware shop. Straight ahead only 100 yards or so along the village street, our visitor could call at another inn – The Red Lion - before admiring first a terrace of small houses, behind and beyond which still rises a succession of major dwellings housing the moneyed families of the village leading to the really spacious halls of the local nobility displayed in our picture gallery.

Originally the first Coop store in Longton opposite the Golden Ball

Beyond the village on the Hutton Road the visitor would be surprised by a succession of even grander estates beginning with Longton Hall.

Formerly Manor House, one acre site just developed with nine major houses

Former C of E Rectory
— two large detached houses now occupy part of the huge garden

19th Century doctor's house

Former barn of doctor's house, now large separate dwelling

Booths store on former Mansion House site

Farm house on top of ridge

View from half way across the estuary as at early 19th century.
The globe and other buildings at Warton airfield are just visible.

HESKETH BANK AND TARLETON

The maps of the early 19th century show three villages in a line northwards from the turnpike road, which is now the A59, just before it goes southwards towards Ormskirk, – Tarleton, Becconsall and Hesketh Bank.

Hesketh Bank was originally a narrow strip of houses on land by the very tip of the estuary of the River Douglas as it turned west along to the Ribble. Even today some of the very old properties carry signs demonstrating that they were on the coast. On the 1848 map the line showing the high water mark at spring tides is close along the shore. The title of Bank is clearly related to a sharply sloping strip of ground running down to this line from a high ridge of land on which the houses were built. Close by is Johnson's Ferry. The same map shows a Methodist chapel just behind the coastal strip of houses.

Becconsall was essentially the tiny village close to the River Douglas with two direct ferry connections to Longton and Hoole on the other side. It had its own Ferry House, with the title still showing on a private house next to which there seems once to have been an inn. These were

Becconsall Church

just across the street from the 1765 church with a hall visible over the fields. The church is still maintained by the Church of England but is only used on special occasions.

One of the guides who helped travellers across the river and marshes was James Blundell who died in 1894. The epitaph on his grave-stone in the churchyard says it all;

> Often times I have crossed the sands
> *And through the Ribble deep*
> *But I was found in Astland drown'd*
> *Which caused me here to sleep*
> *It was Gods will it should be so*
> *Some way or other all must go*

Some two miles south of the shore at Hesketh Bank is the village of Tarleton which has enjoyed the benefit of close road access to other places north and south. Both villages also benefited from the improved

navigation of the River Douglas and its connection to the Leeds and Liver-pool Canal, especially following its canalisation. The following table shows how this stimulus increased the local population:-

	Hesketh with Becconsall (as the area became known)	Tarleton
1801	353	1,116
1851	692	1,945
1901	901	1,800

As the River Douglas approaches the Tarleton area from the south-east its extremely curving shape is by-passed by the canal built by the Leeds and Liverpool Canal Company to make it navigable. This canal is joined to the river estuary by a substantial lock, which today still carries a

River Douglas going towards River Ribble from Becconsall

Boat yard at Becconsall by River Douglas going towards Tarleton — a few of the old boats are inhabited

St Michael's church. at Much Hoole

sign of welcome to the "Leeds and Liverpool Canal". (Henceforth in this history we will refer to Hesketh with Becconsall by its modern title of Hesketh Bank).

The lock is approached by a special landing stage, over a quarter of a mile long, where boats both from inland and the Ribble could load and unload their goods. All this shipping activity brought much business and work to both Tarleton and Hesketh Bank which included the maintenance and repair of boats and the handling of goods, so that by 1851 the joint population of the two villages had doubled.

In spite of the great increase in traffic along the River Douglas there is no doubt that the community of people who lived around Hesketh Bank, just like the inhabitants of Longton, continued to make and maintain contact with their neighbours across the river, and the ferry traffic across the Ribble greatly encouraged and assisted contacts in that direction.

On the Longton side of the Douglas there were a number of favoured points of departure to Hesketh Bank, including the one near the ferry house at the end of Marsh Lane and a footpath from Hall Green. About two miles from Longton, on the main road to Tarleton, is the village of Much Hoole, where in the 17th century was built the parish church of St Michael's, where a young schoolteacher helped with services on Sundays. His name was Jeremiah Horrocks. He was a brilliant mathematician and astronomer who became famously able to predict the Transit of Venus. Across the road from this church is a footpath leading to one of the ferry routes to Becconsall and Hesketh Bank. A collection of local oral writings and sayings includes an anonymous poem by a man who must have been a preacher at St Michael's. This poem, which apparently dates from 1887, bears eloquent testimony to the fact that this preacher travelled regularly by ferry from his home on the Becconsall side of the river.

The following is part of the poem –

> *Wandering on Douglas' banks*
> *The autumn breeze bears on its breath*
> *The memories of the past,*
> *Decayed and withered, like the leaves of trees*
> *Soon to be borne upon the wintry blast.*
> *Yon ancient temple by the river's side*
> *Resort of pious souls for many a day;*
> *How oft its bell has rung for blooming bride*
> *And eke how oft has tolled for lifeless clay.*
> *A simple sundial here; the graves among,*
> *Tell us at Becconsall the hours of prayer;*
> *But ever and anon from Hoole is flung*
> *The church clock's chiming on the Sabbath air.*

4.   RAILWAY AGE IN SOUTH RIBBLE

Clearly, by 1887 much had changed. The Ribble had been greatly altered, having become narrower, straighter and deeper, surrounded by marshy land. Perhaps above all, the Railway Age had altered many things. We must tell the story of its local impact on the villages on the south bank of the Ribble estuary.

Preston had of course been an important railway junction since the 1840's. Southport attracted its first line, to Liverpool, in 1848 and its second to Manchester via Wigan in 1855 and finally by a direct line in 1862. In the following decades it attracted huge numbers of visitors from the Lancashire cotton towns, especially for their wakes weeks, even after the sea receded from the 1870's. It might have seemed that there was enough wealth in Southport to support a direct line to Preston even though it could be reached via Wigan. The commercial case for such a line always, however, seemed dubious since only a few people lived between the two major towns and there was little industry. The people of Preston itself could very easily travel to Lytham and Blackpool by train, and St Annes grew as a new seaside resort from the 1870's.

It is not, therefore, altogether surprising that an initiative by Southport businessmen, which began in the 1860's with an aborted parliamentary bill, could lead to a Southport to Preston line being completed only in 1882. The first stage was opened on 19th February 1878 from Hesketh Park in Southport to Hesketh Bank by the Ribble. The opening ceremony in Hesketh Park, which was attended by the Mayors of Preston and Blackburn, was serenaded by the Rifle Volunteer Band. Two trains ran on the opening journeys, one of them notably named "Sir Thomas Fermor Hesketh" (the owner of land over a huge area around), but later re-named "Longton".

There had originally been a proposal to carry livestock and goods onwards from Hesketh Bank on steam vessels on the Rivers Douglas and Ribble to Preston, Lytham, Blackpool, Fleetwood and even the Isle of Man and indeed to anywhere on the Leeds Liverpool Canal. This somewhat fantastical plan was not achieved, partly no doubt because the existing main railway development had already taken so much traffic from both roads and waterways. So the Southport line was finally extended to Preston in 1880-82, a project which involved building a swing bridge over the River Douglas. The great investment confidence among businessmen in the mid-Victorian period had responded to the use of the line to Hesketh Bank being below expectations by proceeding with the extension to Preston, which did indeed bring about an improvement. Thus the number of trains a day, which had been cut from 12 to 6 a day, was restored to 12 a day when the Preston connection was made.

The railway swing bridge over the River Douglas at Becconsall

Towards the end of the century the full list of stations was:

> Southport Central
> Windsor Road
> Hesketh Park
> Churchtown
> Crossens
> Banks
> Hundred End Gate
> Hesketh Bank

(with branch to Tarleton by the River Douglas)

> Hoole
> Longton
> Howick (later New Longton)
> Penwortham
> Preston (Fishergate Hill)

The total journey time was 45 minutes for stopping trains but there were some expresses. Fares for the whole journey were:

> 1st class   3s 9d (19p)
> 2nd class   2s 8d (13p)
> 3rd class   2s 0d (10p)

The arrival of the railway undoubtedly constituted a revolution for Hesketh Bank and Longton, radically reducing the social isolation which they had endured until then and which had driven local people to make difficult and sometimes dangerous crossings over their two commercially important rivers. This revolution did not come too soon since the development of the Ribble in particular made it difficult to cross over sandy marshes and a deep and swiftly flowing channel. In any event, as we know of the 1887 poem quoted above, "the ferryman now plies his trade no more".

The expense of using the train even for connections to close villages was of course not inconsiderable. The luxury of an occasional trip to Southport or to the Fylde coast was not easy to afford for the many work-people earning less than £1 a week and in the late 19th century was obviously expensive, but it would become a more regular attraction as wages improved in the 20th century. With the average distances between stations less than 1½ miles it was something like a bus system before its time!

Of course, the railroad network made a major contribution to trade and industry by providing alternative methods of transport with growing competition between them. As we have seen, the most striking local advantage from the rail link at Longton related to the extensive quarrying of brick clay and the manufacture of bricks and tiles close to the station on

Originally the Railway Inn - now The Becconsall

the Liverpool Road in Longton which acquired a special siding for the despatch of products.

At Hesketh Bank, or rather at Becconsall, a brick works also had been established in 1877, just before the railway arrived, by the young Henry Alty who had gained experience of the industry at Burscough. Presumably Mr Alty had got wind of the plan to open the railway line and decided to take advantage of this novel and very effective way of sending

bricks to customers over a wide area. Of course the brick works acquired its own siding running into the railway.

Even before this facility became available, Mr Alty used his own boat to move a large proportion of his output across the Ribble to Lytham where it constituted most of the material for the extensive construction as

Mr Alty's boat providing a shuttle service, carrying bricks to Lytham

the town grew quickly in the mid-Victorian period. It seems that this business owed much to Mr Alty's wife who had important contacts in Lytham.

The fact that the brick works closed in 1965, just after the railway was closed, was apparently just a coincidence since the company's problems stemmed from the increased competition from brickworks elsewhere using higher quality clay. There was also a reduction in the general demand for bricks as breeze blocks became more popular. These problems were depressingly similar to those affecting the Longton brickworks on a similar timescale.

After the brickworks closed, the company developed a business of the distribution of building materials which has continued into the 21st century. The current turnover of the company is some £8m per annum. Only a

third is for building materials, the remainder for horticultural products, in spite of the general loss of business in horticulture to Holland and other continental countries.

Two years after the closure of the brickworks, six schoolboys established the West Lancashire Light Railway on the site – a working museum for preserving and operating 2ft gauge locomotives and rolling stock – which still thrives in 2008. On many Sundays through most of the year, little trains are run for families to the old quarry, from which the clay was dug for the brickworks.

The traffic on the Rivers Douglas and Ribble, which in mid-century had seen some 300 vessels a year at Hesketh Bank and Tarleton causing local populations to double in the first half of the century, had subsided. In the second half of the century, however, Hesketh with Becconsall increased from 700 to 900, no doubt because of the stimulus of the railway, whilst Tarleton declined from 1,945 to 1,800 despite having a branch freight line from Becconsall to its riverside loading area. There was also an attempt to join the two areas together with the main station name changed from Hesketh Bank to Tarleton, but this was defeated by noisy opposition.

It appears that the general prospects for the Hesketh Bank area were so attractive at the time of the First World War that Sir Thomas Hesketh the chief landowner, decided to raise funds by selling a substantial area around the village, including the main street area then known as Hesketh Lane but now named Station Road. A substantial part of this central area, some 40 acres, was purchased by Mr Henry Alty the brick maker, and a smaller area by a Southport businessman. Together they developed a plan for building seven new streets with some 70 houses, supposedly 'villa residences'. Mr Alty himself organised the building of a row of

Houses built by Mr Alty

houses along Station Road close to the brickworks. Certainly Hesketh Bank continued to expand in the Age of the Train and even into the Age of the Car with its population rising by 50% in the first half of the 20th century and even accelerating thereafter.

Nevertheless the Age of the Train did witness the arrival of a limited amount of industry to Tarleton, first a textile mill at the end of the 19th century and, after the first world war, a weaving mill close to the canal and its landing stage at what was then known as Town End but today is called Plox Brow, which has become a small industrial area. Its approach road from the village boasts some of the oldest houses in the area.

In the 21st century, Tarleton remains an attractive small town in a basically agricultural area which has been successful in persuading the authorities to build a new road from the A565 running towards Southport to enable heavy traffic to travel to and from the town area without disturbing the modern residential areas.

The Cock & Bottle in Tarleton village

Tarleton's elegant square

The smaller villages around also benefited from the railway. In the greater Longton area the population had stagnated in the middle of the 19th century, even falling to a low of 2,706 in 1891 but increasing after that to 3,250 in 1901 and 3,985 by 1911.

The story of New Longton is particularly interesting. The village stands some 1½ miles from the centre of Longton, some half a mile beyond the Chapel Street end of the Long Town. The Preston line railway on its way from Longton to Penwortham and Preston was obliged to run close to what was really no more than a hamlet, so much so that the station was originally called Howick and Hutton, both of which are well over a mile away. The presence of this little station on the line to Preston and Southport encouraged the building of a long line of substantial houses along the road back towards Longton so that the Long Town of continuous housing now extends to nearly three miles with a short break along Chapel Lane on the New Longton side of the modern by-pass road which does break its continuity.

The story of New Longton is mirrored to some extent by that of Hoole, where a station was placed in the countryside between Hesketh Bank and Longton. In the following decade or so some 20 modest semi-

detached houses sprang up and subsequently a similar number of larger houses were built, all because of the convenience of the railway station. Altogether the populations of Much Hoole and Little Hoole rose from 567 and 431 in 1891 to 624 and 501respectively in 1901.

Of course, the railway s crossing of the River Douglas in 1882, although relieving the relative isolation of Hesketh Bank people to some extent, jumped a mile or two in each direction, so by-passing the close neighbours who in earlier years had met by foot or ferry across the river. Even the railway had been closed by Beeching in the 1960s. However in 2008 a new plan has been developed for constructing a foot and cycle bridge from Becconsall to the somewhat deserted area across the Douglas towards the old church at Much Hoole. A competition organised by Lancashire County Council has produced the elegant design in our picture. All that is now required is for the local councils to raise some £3m to achieve a notable improvement to encourage local walkers and cyclists to explore and enjoy the unspoilt countryside across the river—and to meet more neighbours and even walk to church!

5.   THE NORTH BANK OF THE RIBBLE ESTUARY

LYTHAM ST ANNES

Clearly, the north bank of the estuary has important characteristics in common with the south bank. Both areas are quite isolated from the rest of Lancashire with Preston as their nearest town, now a city. Their exposure to the Irish Sea and the often dominant west wind bring similarities of climate with dramatic storms inflicting disastrous blows every few decades. Even Longton had flood water approaching the village in 1927. At the very tip of the estuary the ancient town of Lytham has always been particularly exposed to the west wind. In the 11th century it appears that a moderately high tide backed by a storm wind uprooted banks of trees on the coast and then buried them deep in sand so that they were not unearthed for centuries. A few miles north the resort of Blackpool has in modern times been notorious for its winter winds and in 2008 a sizeable ship has been lying crippled on the beach.

In spite of its weather, this exposed corner of England has for many

centuries been the home for many more people than its neighbours on either side of the Ribble. This is essentially because of its weather-defying history and its seaside position. It all started in the 12th century when Benedictine monks from Durham started a Norman Priory roughly where Lytham Hall now stands, which was for centuries a target for pilgrims and monks crossing from Hesketh Bank. The property was taken over by King Henry VIII when he dissolved the monasteries in the 1530's and passed through various hands until it was bought by the Clifton famil᠄ in 1606. The total estate covered 16,000 acres and the Cliftons effectivel᠄ owned all the land far around Lytham. They lived a highly privileged anc eccentric life around the world on the rents of the land, mainly from farm-ing ,until Harry, the last of the line, squandered £3½ million pounds in 3C years, ending in bankruptcy and the sale of the estate in 1963. A donatior of almost £1 million pounds by BAE Systems (see our chapter on Warton᠄ enabled the estate to be devoted to public use. The present noble Jaco-bean Hall was built by John Carr of York between 1752 and 1764.

Lytham Hall

Until recent decades the Hall and the Estate blocked residential and other development to the north of the town of Lytham, so encouraging the construction of housing to the west towards St Annes and the develop-ment of the whole of Ansdell. A large south-west area of the former Park itself is now a considerable residential area called South Park.

On the tip of the estuary, Lytham has in fact been favoured in some respects. After all, it does not face directly west into the strongest winds as St Annes, its modern offshoot, does. By the same token, nature long ago endowed Lytham with Lingard Creek which drained water from its hin-terland flowing westwards into a sheltered pool forming a large natural dock. The Manor of Lytham historically owned the water rights around the shore and fought battles with local ship owners, including those from Pre-ston, seeking to avoid paying tolls to the Lord of the Manor.

It appears that in 1830 one observer commented that the Pool was wide enough to harbour a fleet of warships – but of course warships were not so large in those days! Certainly this was a local advantage for the north bank of the Ribble estuary, which, rather like the creek at Freckleton which we shall consider later, to some extent matched the benefits of the River Douglas at Hesketh Bank to the south. As shipping increased in the early 19th century, the advantage of a good natural dock inspired the Lord of the Manor to build a proper shipping dock in the Lytham Pool.

The problems which the Preston ship owners, organised in conjunction with the Ribble Navigation Company, were having in improving the river led them to take over the Lytham Dock in 1841 and invest in its substantial improvement so as it became a convenient transit facility where ships could rest when tides were not propitious for getting directly into or out of Preston, often unloading or loading cargoes. The changes made up to this time and for some decades afterwards by dredging and channelling the river brought the deeper main channel close to Lytham dock, so enhancing its value to Preston. By mid-century some 500 ships a year were going to or past Lytham, many of them using it as a port.

Indeed, it has been suggested that if a number of the more important businesses of the early 19th century had ventured to invest substantially in Lytham dock, instead of spending such vast sums on improving the Ribble, Preston Dock could have been superseded. Be that as it may, the Ribble Navigation Company had itself so clearly perceived the great usefulness of the Lytham Dock. This was its golden age.

Ships were getting even bigger and it is difficult to believe that a great wet dock as large as that in which the Preston council had to invest in the 1880's, could have been built at Lytham. In any event the strenuous efforts to make the Ribble more navigable up to Preston themselves moved the main channel somewhat away from the shore at Lytham to the great disadvantage of its dock so that after 1880 it effectively became a haven only for small boats. In the 20th century worse was to follow as Lytham eventually lost its attractive beach and the new resort of St Annes saw its pier become somewhat high and dry – all because of the changes men had made to the Ribble.

Until the late 19th century period, of course, Lytham, like the other Ribbleside places had been greatly involved in cross-river traffic. It was always a favoured north bank point of departure and arrival, alongside Warton and ahead of the Naze at Freckleton, for fording on foot and especially on ferries. By 1880 the major changes in the Ribble and especially the deepening and increased flow in the re-organised main channel made crossing even by boat, let alone on foot, very much more difficult.

Of course, the arrival of the railways in the 1840's, earlier than on the south bank where the Southport to Preston line did not open until 1882, provided alternative means of transport, although never across the Ribble estuary. From the industrial areas of Lancashire, near Wigan and elsewhere, there were from the 1840's train routes via Preston as well as a much earlier canal route which we shall explain later.

In short, on foot or by ferry, it was much more unusual to cross the estuary as the 19th century wore on because of the deepening and divert-

Lytham Beach—early 20th century.

ing of the river and of other methods of travel which progressively took over.

Although the dock at Lytham, with some ship building, remained of significance for a long time yet, the town had other strings to its bow in the form of the seaside holiday trade, which had begun even in the early years of the 19th century and grown so much by the 1870's, both at Blackpool and Lytham, that a new resort of St Annes could be founded between them from 1875, as we shall see. By this time Southport on the other tip of the Ribble estuary, had grown into a major wealthy Victorian resort patronised by the industrial rich and factory poor. We must trace the growth of the holiday trade by the north bank of the Ribble.

At this point, however, it is appropriate to recall a major distinction of Lytham compared to the villages on the south bank. Longton was somewhat unusual in that it had no local Lord of the Manor. Hesketh Bank had a major local landowner in Sir Thomas Hesketh, but he had no local residence. Since the 17th century however, Lytham had the Clifton family, as Lords of the manor, owning Lytham Hall, a Georgian mansion. The head of the family was generally an important leader in local life, being involved, as we have explained, in the building of the dock. His support was essential in the 1820's for the scheme for making the water front into an esplanade or public walk along the crest of the beach. The Cliftons' grip on

The Clifton Arms Hotel looking towards Southport

Lytham's 200 year old windmill set in the park in front of the Clifton Arms

The view to Southport five miles across the estuary. Note the rough area in the fore-ground where the beach was a century ago

land tenure had to be loosened for the development of the land with buildings for the modern age.

By this time the population of the village reached over 1,200 and several hotels had been built together with fine taverns. Sea bathing had already become something of a craze for seaside people and others who could travel by stagecoach or canal to a seaside town. Far across at the other edge of the estuary visitors were arriving at Churchtown hotels for a similar reason, but the sea had already begun to recede so a local hotelier early in the century built a modest hostelry on the coast, so founding the great resort of Southport.

This new pastime of sea bathing raised something of a decency problem for men and women enjoying it together even in voluminous costumes. At Lytham this was for a time resolved by having a bell rung as the tide came in to warn the men to leave the beach to the ladies for an hour or two until the tide had well turned when the men could reclaim possession. Times were indeed changing in front of the Clifton Arms Hotel.

As we have seen, the early growth of Southport was greatly stimulated in the early decades of the 19th century by the arrival of the Leeds and Liverpool Canal at Scarisbrick, barely five miles away, on its way to Liverpool, opening a canal route to Manchester by 1820 as well as to major industrial towns like Blackburn and Wigan. From a wide area, visitors to Southport were able to travel by canal boat to Scarisbrick (if they could afford it, as many cotton industrialists and managers could), and transfer to horse-drawn carriages and carts for the five mile trip to the seaside.

Lytham had no need of such a canal connection, although the Lancaster Canal came quite close and there was once an aborted plan for building one to Preston to avoid the difficult transit of the Ribble. The river was in any event a major access route for small passenger boats to come to the seaside. By 1830 two packet boats regularly carried people on the trip from Preston, which of course was soon to become a major railway junction.

The demand for such journeys was so great that in 1846 the railway came to Lytham with a line from Preston via Kirkham. In the same year Blackpool also rejoiced at its first line, also a branch of the Wyre to Preston line, which had been originally attracted by the port of Fleetwood. Yet Lytham was not connected to Blackpool until a single line was opened in 1863. A new extension joining the two lines was built in 1874, all "paving the way" for the foundation of St Annes on Sea, to which we shall come later.

This rate of progress in the railway system was not very different from that at the southern side of the Ribble area. For Southport, the first connection to Waterloo did not come until 1848, continuing to Liverpool in 1850. The first connection to Manchester, via Wigan, came in 1855 with a direct line opening in 1862. As we have seen, a line to Preston took until

1882.

St Annes was in fact founded in 1875 by a group of cotton magnates from Rawtenstall who saw the opportunity for providing a somewhat up-market alternative to Blackpool which was already becoming a favourite target for trippers from the Lancashire factories. Lytham was itself becoming quite crowded in the area close to the water, limited by the configuration of its promenade, the park of Lowther Gardens, and some elevated land round the corner towards Blackpool. Additional residential building inland was constricted by the huge grounds of Lytham Hall so that new houses to the north were squeezed into areas becoming further and further from the beach.

There was, however, ample room for expansion to the north-west around the corner of the land with over four miles of sand hills stretching to the South Shore of Blackpool. The original lease of land from the Clifton family to the St Annes' on the Sea Land and Building Company was centred on the coast about 2½ miles from Lytham and covered some 80 acres stretching about half a mile along the coast and a similar distance inland. The area was later extended to 600 acres. Clearly there was the most ample space for the continuing expansion of the new resort area.

The original prospectus of the company read as follows:-

"Of late years, Blackpool has become so much the resort of excursionists that a decided want is felt for a watering place, which while possessing the same bracing atmosphere and commanding position on the coast as Blackpool, shall secure a more select, better class of visitors. The favourable circumstances under which the company commences operations, the whole of the land being under one control and there being no fishermen's huts or unhealthy dwellings to remove, and no bad system of drainage to eradicate, will combine to make St Annes' on Sea one of the healthiest, neatest and most cleanly watering places. The land possesses elements certain to ensure its development, the well-known salubrity of its climate, the nature and dryness of its subsoil and the ready and direct access it commands by means of the new railway with the manufacturing districts of Lancashire and Yorkshire, will render it equally popular with many other of the seaside resorts for which the west coast is so noted and justify the belief that the land will afford a fine opportunity for successful building operations."

The confidence expressed in this prospectus was well justified. The other resorts it mentioned of course included Southport, which had already exploded at the estuary's southern end. Most strikingly well timed for St Annes' just round the northern tip, Southport was just experiencing its first major setback in the form of the retreat of the sea remarkably caused by the same man-made changes to the Ribble itself which would soon damage Lytham and later cause some problems for the expansion of St Annes'. More immediately, however, Southport's new handicap would offer a timely bright light to the already attractive prospect of success for St Annes.

It was of course the arrival of the railway which most notably encouraged the growth of the population of Lytham from only some 3,000 people in 1861 to 8,000 in 1871. For decades there was relative stagnation as the new development of St Annes attracted nearly all the new arrivals. By 1901 the combined total in the two resorts had topped 14,000 rising quite remarkably to 19,200 by 1911 with St Annes already just overtaking its older sister town. When the two towns were joined in the Royal Borough in 1922 their joint population had risen to some 26,000, a level at which it stagnated for many years, only rising substantially after the second of the two world wars. In the inter-war period, which was nationally a very difficult economic period, there was of course strong competition from long established Blackpool.

By this time the country was well into the Age of the Car and beginning to experience the Age of Flight. We shall need to consider how the whole Ribble Estuary area fared in the new world.

The Lytham dock never recovered from the deadly blow of the desertion of the main Ribble channel. As we have seen, even Preston Dock had to struggle for survival in the modern world. A large area of land at Lytham became available for other uses, with housing attractively available at St Annes. So various industrialists took over the dock area, which was in any event just outside the main existing residential area of Lytham. As a first notable step Richard Smith transferred his well-known shipbuilding yard from Preston to Lytham Dock in 1888.

Towards the end of the first World War two large sheds were erected for the assembly of Felixstowe flying boats built by the Dick, Kerr & Co / English Electric Company at Strand Road in Preston. These sheds were used for the final manufacture and assembly of other light aircraft including flying boats made mainly by Fairey Engineering and English Electric until 1926. Subsequently the hangars were taken over by a film company and in 1930 part of the complex was demolished with one of the hangars being taken over by the new Cookson bakery which expanded and occupied a major part of the whole site for some 70 years.

Closer to the actual dock a variety of engineering operations, including some shipbuilding, persisted over a similar period.

For commercial purposes of any substantial scale, marketing access became something of a problem in the modern age. Trains served passengers pretty well and a motorway (the M55) was built connecting the M6 almost to Blackpool. For the substantial movement of goods, however, road transport remained vital and local road connections from Lytham re-

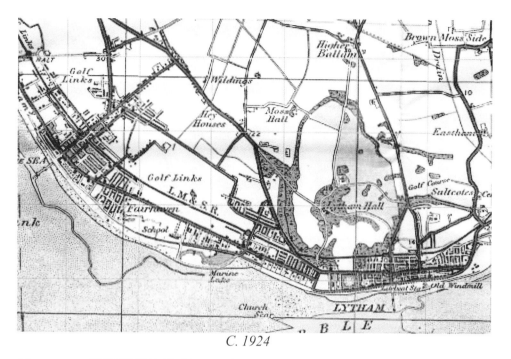

C. 1924

C. 2004

mained rather poor. Even the railway was not much help in carrying goods to England, east of Preston.

Thus, like other areas around the Ribble estuary, the principal investment opportunities were residential since people could increasingly travel by car and so live significant distances from their work. In a more affluent age many people could afford new modern houses in areas which were attractive places to live in. The south-eastern Fylde was undoubtedly among these areas, especially with the advantage of the proximity of Preston, growing to become a city.

The demand for more housing in the Lytham area, after even St Annes had somewhat filled up, was met by two substantial estates on the St Annes side of Lytham, as well as the large corner of the Lytham Hall estate which we have mentioned. One of these was Cypress Point by the

Pleasant sitting area in the middle of Lytham. The river is only 100 yards or so to the left

Lytham's busy attractive main shopping street.

Blackpool Road to the west beyond Lytham Hall Park where Kensington Developments, a major house building company, built some 600 homes.

One of a number of large impressive houses on the Lytham Quays estate.

2008 view from top floor of large house on Lytham Quays.
Note small stream close to development with main river some distance beyond.

To the east, however, in the old dock area and beyond, no significant housing development took place until very recently.

Early in the 21st century, as the industrial occupants of the old dock area were finding business somewhat difficult, Kensington Developments proposed to build several thousand houses of a high-density character there, but local opposition was fierce and planning permission was not forthcoming, partly no doubt because of the traffic problems. Eventually the company was more successful with a project for some 260 high quality houses in the south-western section of the old dock area designated as Lytham Quays, formerly the site of Cooksons bakery, with individual house values up to £2 million each. By the end of 2008 construction of this attractive development was substantially complete.

For this attractive estate the company has in fact created its own environment with views over the estuary as far as Southport and with easy access to the many shops and civic communities of old Lytham. The nearby creek is still bringing water from the mainland to the Ribble estuary, as it did for the Lytham Dock and the development is planning to construct a second phase project close to the remaining water on a somewhat

Another view on the Lytham Quays estate - a large apartment block under construction. An office of the Land Agency is visible in the near distance

smaller area of land, but involving rather more properties of a more modest character.

These two phases of developments have been significantly slowed down by the depressed state of the housing market from the spring of 2008, but could well increase the Lytham population by more than 1,000 people over a period of four or five years. This growth should be good news for local shops particularly the Booths grocery chain which has maintained small shops in Lytham and St Annes, as well as in Ansdell, in the long period since opening one first in Lytham in 1879. In 2007 the company opened a major new supermarket on the site of the first railway station in Haven Road, which is linked to a new branch of Stringers, the local department store. The Booths store is uniquely designed to fit with its seaside setting. The company is retaining its smaller stores in the local shopping areas in competition with several other similar sized shops, al-though the original tiny one in Lytham has recently been closed.

Booths also have popular stores on the south bank of the Ribble. As we have seen, the typically comfortable sized one in the middle of Longton maintains a tradition going back over eighty years on three differ-ent sites leading to the present one where a mansion house stood ten years ago. It has a sister store only two miles away in Penwortham. Just a few miles west along the Ribble the company have acquired a site at Hesketh Bank, also an important area in this book, where a new store will be opened in a year or so. Clearly Booths are quite a Ribble company.

FRECKLETON

Freckleton lies on the north bank of the Ribble estuary, directly opposite Hesketh Bank but somewhat closer to Longton because of the shape of the land. It has always been comparably isolated from the rest of Lancashire like its neighbours across the river, but similarly also within a long walk of Preston. Its comparative isolation has however been somewhat mitigated by the towns of the Fylde with Kirkham and Lytham quite close, more substantial places than the villages to the south of the river.

We already know of course that there were frequent and varied connections across the Ribble in its shallow meandering state of the 18th and early 19th centuries, with ford paths at low tide from Hesketh Bank and Longton. A mile or so north-east of Longton towards Hutton an old road goes off north-west, known as Skip Lane, where legend has it children skipped across to the ford towards Freckleton. On the way to the river is an old guide house which has been modernised.

Freckleton has no substantial river running close to compare with Hesketh Bank's Douglas, yet it did have the benefit of a minor river called the Don flowing from Kirkham, running by its side and forming a narrow natural harbour alongside The Naze, a promontory standing quite high for about a mile south into the Ribble, provided good natural shelter for boats. Thus Freckleton was from its early days known to have a most useful harbour and in the 18th century the Douglas Navigation ran regular ferries and cargo boats right across to Freckleton as well as to Lytham. Although narrow this harbour has always been known as Freckleton Pool.

There is also evidence that, like Lytham's, Freckleton's harbour was valued as a staging post for Preston for ships which could not make the journey for the full length of the river in one go because of its tidal character. At the beginning of the 19th century some shipping companies quoted carriage charges from Liverpool for various goods, including flax from Ireland, at similar standard rates to Lytham, Freckleton and Preston.

Inevitably, Lytham was more important to the Preston trade because of its more substantial harbour and its position at the mouth of the river. It was therefore the beneficiary of a major improvement project of the Ribble Navigation Company in the early 1840's, but the Leeds and Liverpool Company, after it took the Douglas company over, also undertook some improvement to the Freckleton Quay at around the same time and a coal yard was established soon afterwards. Coal was of course the principally vital cargo.

The result of the work of the Navigation Company was that the Lytham dock and the Ribble channel were so improved that the river traffic, including larger boats, could generally make the journey either directly to Preston or including a stop at Lytham if they did not actually unload there. Thus from the early 1840's the business of the Freckleton dock seriously declined, so that only local boats used it. As we have seen, the Lytham dock suffered a similar fate as a result of the further river "improvements" of early 1880's. By then, of course, the whole area was well into the Age of the Train.

To the east, Freckleton was blessed with a stretch of marsh land, over three miles long, sloping down to the Ribble which was often invaded by high tides and so not capable of being normally cultivated. It was however used by neighbouring farmers for temporary usage such as the feeding of cattle, a precious advantage which had to be controlled and rationed. We have seen that a vast area of the southern estuary was reclaimed after the dredging and controlling of the river by the mid 19th century. The same effect resulted close to the north bank but to a much smaller extent. A modern map shows a strip of well over 3 miles of land east of Freckleton, which was shown as water 200 years ago. Now it is fertile agricultural land boasting two major farms and a sewage works.

Whilst agriculture inevitably remained the chief occupation of the Freckleton area in the 19th century, weaving, mainly in people's homes, struggled to survive as larger factories took over. Other industries played increasing roles, principal among which was ship building which, with the great natural advantage of the local dock, was important from the late 18th century, certainly from the 1780's, and still continues on the Naze today in the form of work on small boats.

Closely connected to ships also, the trade of sail making developed in the Freckleton area from the 18th century, a specialised form of textile weaving. This was facilitated by the easy availability of flax from Ireland and flourished in workshops, factories even, of various sizes. The most notable business was established on the Lytham road early in the 19th century in a substantial building where sacking and sailcloth were produced. This was essentially a weaving factory which eventually included hundreds of looms employing hundreds of people. It became known as Balderstone Mill and appears to have operated more or less continuously for nearly a century and a half until it stuttered to complete closure in 1980, its fate following that of swathes of cotton manufacturers in England in the face of cheap production elsewhere.

In the 19th century, Freckleton remained a smallish village struggling to reach a population of 1,000 from some 560 in 1801. The major setback for the port in the early 1840's must be held responsible for a reduction from 995 in 1841 to 879 in 1861 after which the general growth in the economy and no doubt the expansion of Balderstone Mill floated it up to 1,308 in 1891. This was in spite of the fact that the town did not experience the benefit of the arrival of the railway similar to that experienced by Longton and Hesketh Bank in the early 1880's. In fact the north bank of the Ribble estuary has had no railway connection closer than Lytham or Kirkham.

    This area of land, including a half mile wide strip recovered in the first half of the 19th century was protected by the Freckleton Embankment originally built in 1864.

    The Embankment was breached in 1907 and 1927. In the latter case the damage was mainly to the flanking return on the west, near to the Naze headland, through which successive tides flooded and took out large amounts of soil. About half Freckleton Farm, some 250 acres, was flooded by spring tides until the breach was finally repaired in May 1928.

    From Naze Point, over Freckleton Pool, a piled gantry was made to carry a 2 feet rail track with "Jubilee" wagons to carry clay dug by a steam navvy from the Naze bank across to the breach.

    Indeed, Freckleton had to wait until the 1920's for a regular bus service after the by-pass road to Warton and Lytham was constructed. In the 20th century the most substantial employment boost for Freckleton people came in the Ages of the Car and Flight with war time development at Warton of a military airfield for the American forces followed by the use of the area for military aircraft production by English Electric and later BAE Systems.

    The war period brought a major disaster to Freckleton when in 1944 an American Liberator aircraft was hit by lightning and crashed on to the infants department of Trinity School killing many children and teachers in a total death roll of 61.

Another view of the devastation caused by the great flood.

The Ship Inn as it is today

In spite of the very limited increase in local industrial activity in the first half of the 20th century, the population of Freckleton almost doubled to 2,500 but almost trebled again in the second half of the century, a faster rate than the other places by the Ribble, almost catching up Longton. This great rate of development through the whole area was not the result so much of the growth of local industry or business activity in the towns and

War memorial garden in the middle of Freckleton

The Old Smithy. Prominent feature of the village green from the 19th century. Taken over by the District Bank in 1913.

villages as by the arrival of important companies like British Nuclear Fuels' Springfields plant near Salwick which were within comfortable travelling distance in the Age of the Car, although the airfield at Warton was the huge local exception. The airfield at Warton, a very close neighbour of Freckleton, was of course of major importance to the latter, which we will explain in a separate chapter.

In spite of this latter exception, which was not exactly an attraction for new residents, except as employment, the essential cause of a great increase in modern houses was that Ribbleside, with the sea nearby, was a most pleasant place to live.

The close proximity of Freckleton to the villages on the south bank

View of Ribble (closer) and Douglas close to their junction, taken from near the end of the Naze near Freckleton. There is a glimpse of stream from Freckleton Pool on left.

of the Ribble is brought home to the visitor who walks along the ancient footpath between the west side of the Naze headland and the Pool until, a few hundred yards from the Ribble, he or she can see the confluence of the now slender streams of the Ribble itself and the Douglas with Hesketh Bank in the distance.

WARTON

From time immemorial until the Second World War, Warton was just a tiny village of a few hundred people on the road from Preston to Lytham an agriculture dominated area, just beyond Freckleton, where a road from Kirkham joined the main road. We have noted the principal physical development in the history of the area which was the addition to its usable land in the form of a strip some three miles long by half a mile wide reclaimed from the Ribble, mainly east of Freckleton, as a result of the dredging and channelling of the river in the mid 19th century. This acquisition of very usable land served to emphasise the local dominance of agriculture.

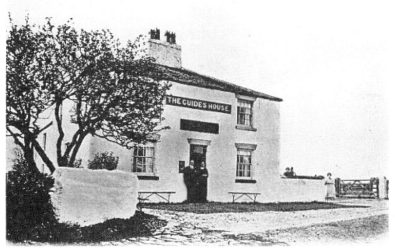

The Guides House Hotel. In the 19th century this was The Guides House, the home of the man who helped people crossing the river on foot or by boat.

Until the 1860's Warton was one of the best places on the north bank of the Ribble from which to walk across the river to Hesketh Bank, to the point that there was a special Guide House for the men who helped people to make the crossing at low tide. Later the journey became more and more dangerous because of the realigning and deepening of the main river channel. By the 1880's fording of the river was effectively at an end.

Early in the Second World War, the British Government searched hard for new military airports in places where the land and terrain were suitable and the population small, so that very few people would have to be uprooted. The reclaimed land, alongside what was known much earlier as Freckleton Marsh, appeared at first to be the ideal choice in the south Fylde area, but examination showed it to be not firm enough, presumably because much of it had previously been marsh.

Just to the west, however and close to Warton was a considerable area with fewer residents which had undoubtedly been solid ground for centuries. It had the additional advantage of standing rather high above the water, particularly at the Naze near Freckleton. The shape of the site was very suitable for an aircraft runway from east to west. The main road to Lytham, close to which most of the people lived, provided good access for workpeople and vehicles. So the land between the inhabited area of Warton and the river to the south was chosen as one of the new military airfields and in 1940 the RAF laid three runways for emergency purposes.

Aerial view of the airfield looking west

The United States of America joined the war late in 1941 as the direct result of the Japanese attack on Hawaii. In the spring of 1942 it was allocated the new airfield site at Warton for its massive air force requirements. People and equipment began to arrive in August, much of them via Liverpool, and a huge transport effort brought the total of personnel over 10,000 by March 1943. In the next three years a truly massive and intense effort earned the site the title of the Greatest Air Depot in the World.

A total of over 14,000 military planes were modified or repaired, including over 4,000 P5s Mustangs and almost 3,000 B524 Liberators with many more planes simply inspected and over 6,000 engines completely overhauled.

Normally the workforce of over 10,000 was divided into three shifts but for a long particularly demanding period in 1944 most staff were required to work 12 hours a day for 7 days a week but eventually were allowed a day a week off. By the winter of 1944 to 1945 when the decisive battles for Western Europe and Germany were being fought, following the

Allied invasion across the channel, the losses of military personnel were so serious that, with the aircraft work at Warton becoming a little less crucial, many of the American workers were transported to the fighting forces on the continent.

The accommodation of these great numbers of aircraft workers was of course a major problem. In the first winter of 1942-43, many of them had to live in tents, suffering cold and inclement weather to which most of them were unaccustomed. A great number of huts had to be erected, many of them in the Freckleton area, since most of the available land in Warton was taken up by the airport itself.

After the end of the war in August 1945, the Americans set up a Training School which, in the period to January 1946 provided training for civilian life for 4,000 of the air force before they went back home. Clearly it was impossible to ship or fly all the many thousands of people back to the U.S.A. in a shorter period. Before many of them left, they attended a memorial service in a new playground in Freckleton dedicated to the memory of the 61 people who died in the disaster of September 1944.

The American 'invasion' had obviously constituted an immense new experience to the south-west shore area of the Fylde, including particularly the entertainment area around Blackpool which enjoyed a huge boost to its income. Many romantic experiences and marriages resulted, with more than a few 'fatherless' children. Nothing faintly like it had been experienced before but it would be recalled soon afterwards when much smaller numbers of RAF people would come soon to use the valuable airport and have the benefit of the accommodation in a multitude of huts.

Altogether the friendly American invasion left a very considerable heritage, which would eventually tempt major private industrial companies to make good use of the most valuable legacy not only of physical items but also of substantial exposure to aircraft technology. In 1945, however, it was inevitably the RAF which took back possession of Warton airfield. Not surprisingly there were few immediate uses which could occupy the huge hangars and workshops which had been built for a massive war effort by 10,000 Americans. For some years the site was mainly used as an RAF storage unit and one of the hangars became a workshop for the repair and maintenance of ground transport.

From 1947 however the English Electric Company began to take over Warton airfield bit by bit, becoming the sole occupant by 1951 and eventually buying it completely from the Aviation Ministry. The company had been involved in the design and production of aircraft since the end of the First World War and during the Second War had built nearly 3,000 Handley Page bombers. Towards the end of the war, the company returned to designing its own bombers, specifically the Canberra, Britain's first jet bomber, much of the development work being undertaken at the company's plants at Preston and Samlesbury.

The Pickwick Tavern next door to the entrance to the huge BAE Systems factory.

Eventually much of the final design, assembly and flight testing work was transferred to Warton which had the advantage of a longer runway than Samlesbury which, even so, had to be extended. This all involved the building of a huge structural test track and two innovative wind tunnels in turn. The site now occupies 283 hectares, the equivalent of something approaching 150 football pitches. In over 300 buildings there are some 7,000 employees on site, not as many as the Americans during the war but they were mainly employed on three shifts. Inevitably these present staff must live over quite a wide area since the village of Warton houses only some 3,500 in all. Clearly Freckleton, the close neighbour village, must house a substantial number, a fact which largely accounts for its great rise in population in the post-war period.

In more recent years English Electric became British Aerospace, which in 1999 merged with part of GEC to form BAE Systems. Its great military aircraft factory and runway occupies almost all of the natural land between the old village of Warton and the Ribble, pushing housing expansion across the main Lytham road.

6.   THE LANCASTER CANAL

We have learnt how the great Leeds and Liverpool Canal was vitally involved in the carriage of coal from the Lancashire mines via Wigan to West Lancashire and beyond, taking over the River Douglas Navigation late in the 18th century so as to export coal through the port of Hesketh Bank. Some of this coal no doubt went to Lancashire, north of the Fylde and indeed to Lancaster and the surrounding area. It is hardly possible to overstate the importance of coal in heating homes and other buildings even before the Age of Steam. It was, after all, this vital requirement which led the Duke of Bridgewater to build the first canal from his coal mine at Worsley, west of Manchester, to the city as early as 1760.

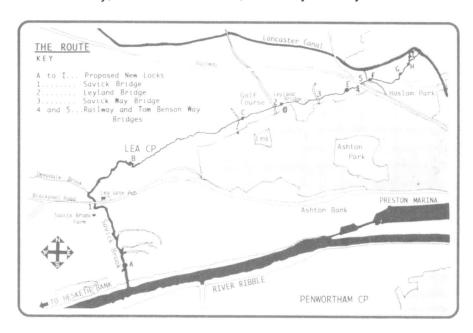

So it is understandable that business people of north Lancashire determined that they needed a more direct route by canal from Wigan which did not need to go round by sea and which would compete effectively with the Leeds and Liverpool. So in 1792 the Lancashire Canal Company was formed with the objective of building a canal from Wigan to Kendal.

The first part of this canal was completed, north from Preston, to Tewitfield just south of Kendal, by 1797, followed in 1799 by the section from Wigan to Chorley, extended by 1803 to Walton Summit, near the south of Preston.

In order to cross the river Ribble close to Preston, the original plan was to build an aqueduct but this proved to be too difficult and expensive. The route from Walton Summit south of Preston, to the Ribble and beyond to the Preston Basin at Ashton to the north, was in any event quite difficult with its variable heights. The only way of crossing this area was determined to be a horse drawn tramway. This was, of course, a long century before the passenger trams which became popular in towns in the 20th century, but the use of rails for modest goods transport pulled by horses had been developed long before the steam driven railways.

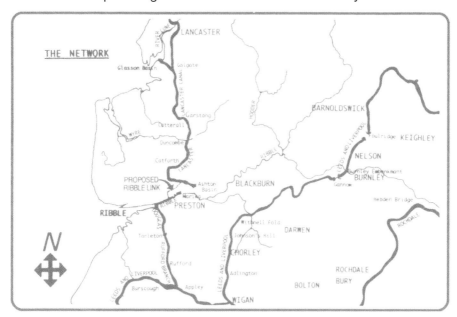

The most difficult part of the journey was across the Ribble Valley. Quite a steep slope down to the river at old Penwortham was difficult enough, but to the north to Avenham the land rose sharply and horse power had to be augmented by a mechanical lift to carry the metal boxes up to the area close to the end of the Avenham colonnade before the horse track turned left to the west near Ribblesdale Place and eventually to a tunnel underneath Fishergate. From its early days the lift was driven by a steam engine as shown in our picture overleaf which also shows the Tower House where the founder of the Booths grocery company lived late in the 19th century.

It seems doubtful however whether steam power could have originally been used to drive the lift at its first operation at the very beginning of the century. It is conceivable that the same horses which pulled the trams along the ground track could have also been pressed into operating a 'treadmill' to lift them up the Avenham slope, just as other horses did in the very early cotton spinning mills such as those devised by Richard Arkwright late in the 18th century before steam engines were invented.

By the 1860's the Lancaster Canal faced powerful competition not only from the Leeds Liverpool Canal, but also from the railways, so that the Preston area tram link scheme was abandoned. Transport business on the River Douglas also suffered, of course, as the Age of the Train took over.

There has recently been a somewhat ironical, even amusing, sequel to the 19th century story. A group known as the Ribble Link Trust Ltd has finally linked the Lancaster Canal to the main canal network by utilising the Savick Brook from the Lancaster Canal, north of Preston, to the Ribble estuary, one and a half miles downstream from Preston Riversway. The new route is along the Ribble westwards for 3½ miles to the River Douglas and then a further four miles to the lock at Tarleton and thus to the Leeds and Liverpool Canal. A Heritage Park is being created along the new route over the land section, planned to be a major tourist attraction.

So, after more than a century of effective separation the two banks of the Ribble estuary have been joined again, as the major old canal competitors, the Leeds and Liverpool and the Lancaster Canals have effectively buried the hatchet implicit in their former rivalry.

7.   CONCLUSIONS

In the 19th century the lives of the folk who lived by the Ribble Estuary were substantially conditioned by the impact of the two rivers, the Ribble and the Douglas. In part, this was in respect of there being barriers to contact and trade with the near neighbours across the water. More powerfully, however, the rivers brought valuable business not only with other parts of England but with other lands. As local barriers they were for long years just challenges to local people who regularly found ways of crossing them on foot or small boats.

During the 19th century the strenuous efforts of ambitious Preston traders and rapacious landowners in dredging and channelling the river, savagely sabotaged the trade of the Estuary ports as well as the opportunities for trading across the Ribble. Gradually and somewhat indirectly, the railways offset these setbacks by providing alternative routes for both trade and people.

By the 20th century neither river mattered very much to their close inhabitants. With cars as well as trains and the planes, as well as huge developments in industry and trade, the Ribble was no more than an increasingly difficult and unimportant route to Preston which ended with the closure of the dock a quarter of a century ago. People came to live by the Ribble essentially because it was quite a pleasant place although there was one major exception to that rule, on the north bank.

In the meantime the south bank had benefited from just a little industry in the shape mainly of two brickworks which lasted as long as the railway which on the north bank only brought people on their way to the sea by the west coast. Longton boasted also a modest weaving mill and two breweries, but they did not thrive long into the 20th century as larger scale industry took over.

The south bank lacked good beaches by the sea as its coastline moved out into the sea itself, most dramatically and disastrously, away from Southport.

The north bank benefited from significant industry from a mill at Freckleton, matching the one at Walmer Bridge, Longton, until well into the 20th century and, later, most significantly, from the replacement of the Lytham dock with a great bakery and various engineering establishments including shipbuilding. All these have been or are, in the 20th and 21st centuries, being replaced by housing.

The one great exception to the foregoing summary of the slow modulation of life by the Estuary has been the massive incursion of industry on the north bank at Warton where BAE systems dominate the scene and provide a major island of industrial employment, essentially because, in the last war, it was a great empty space by the water which was occupied by American military aircraft.

Thus a large aircraft factory has gone some way from the middle of the 20th century to compensate for the progressive economic loss of business as overseas holidays have become more popular and affordable with the blooming growth of holiday flight companies as well as of family incomes. Just inland from the Fylde coast other modern employers such as British Nuclear Fuels continue to provide good quality jobs for the fortunate people who have flocked to live by the river and the sea and use their cars to work even many miles away, whilst the south bank remains closer to Preston and commercial Lancashire.

The whole of the Estuary land remains a good place to live.

ACKNOWLEDGEMENTS

The information, both current and historical, which has been incorporated for this book has been gathered from a multitude of sources over recent years. Thus it is not easy to recognise specific sources for major aspects of the Ribble Estuary story. However the following publications are of particular importance in their own fields;

History of the Ribble Navigation, 1938, by James Barron who was its Chief Engineer for many years (lent by Mr Graham Booth).

The History of Freckleton, 2001, by Peter Shakeshaft (purchased from Freckleton Library).

A History of Tarleton and Hesketh Bank, 1990, by J.A. Perkins typescript held in Tarleton Library).

Rage of Sand, 1971, by Gabriel Harrison – The Story of St Annes available in Lytham Library).

Longton in the 19th Century, 2004, by Marjorie Searson (available in Longton Library).

The Clifton Chronicle, 1990 by John Kennedy (Lytham and other Libraries).

Step into the Past, a chronicle of Life in and Around Longton 1800s and 1900s, Sketches in Local History, Researched and Recorded by Jane Ryding Smith (held in Longton Library).

The pictures of the flood in 1929 close to Freckleton were provided by Mr John Tomlinson owner of Marsh Farm, Clifton to whom special thanks are due.

FRANK BAMFORD

A native of the Midlands, Frank Bamford spent his early professional life in the south. After taking an honours degree in Economics with Modern Economic History at London School of Economics, he had a spell in Government Service, including posts as Private Secretary to Ministers. He soon joined the new Atomic Energy Authority before moving to its offshoot British Nuclear Fuels near Warrington where for nearly 20 years he managed a major world-wide export business which won the Queen s Award for Exports in 1980.

Frank frequently visited the BNFL nuclear fuel factory at Springfields which played a major role in the export business because of its excellent engineering technology. He well remembers taking overseas visitors to stay at the Clifton Arms at Lytham and to have lunch at the Ship at Freckleton.

After retirement, Frank played a major role in local affairs in his home town of Altrincham where he was Chairman of the Civic Society and two boards of school governors. He became the leading local historian, writing three books about the area.

After moving in 2000 to Southport, on the tip of the Ribble Estuary, Frank wrote a well received modern history of the resort entitled Back to the Sea . More recently he has published The Story of Booths which has led him to explore the Ribble estuary, where the Company is the leading grocery retailer, from his home in Longton.